Portrait of the Outer Banks

——*A Pictorial Tour*——

Hatteras Lighthouse, 1862

*by Edwin G. Champney, 5th Mass.
Regiment, courtesy of North Carolina
State Archives and Outer Banks
History Center*

Published by Aerial Perspective / 428 Cripps Drive / Mt. Holly / New Jersey 08060

Copyright © 2000

ISBN 0-9660586-3-1

Printed in China

Portrait of the Outer Banks

——A Pictorial Tour——

Photographs by Robert V. Drapala

Written by Torrey Kim

Portrait of the Outer Banks

Ask anyone who has visited the Outer Banks, "What makes it so special?" and you will inevitably hear a longing sigh, followed by, "You just have to go there and see it yourself."

The delicate barrier islands along North Carolina's coast have a hypnotic effect on those who visit. The islands' guests return to the Cape Hatteras National Seashore as frequently as possible. They vow to move there eventually. And when they finally do relocate, they never leave. Except, of course, when Mother Nature asks them to do so.

The 70-mile-long chain of islands known as the Outer Banks shields the North Carolina mainland from the incessant vehemence of the Atlantic. The islands have been reshaped constantly by changes in the weather ever since the last glacial age was coming to a close nearly 10,000 years ago. At that time, sea level was four hundred feet lower than its present level. As the glaciers melted, sand

dunes washed away, flooding low lying lands and creating shallow pools. The isolated dunes that were left behind formed slender barrier islands, so delicate that they drifted approximately forty miles westward as sea levels continued to swell. Even today, the shoreline moves westward at a rate of 50–200 feet per century, and the Atlantic steals fourteen feet of Hatteras Island beach each year.

Before the Outer Banks was discovered as a prime vacation spot, Native Americans walked the shores over one thousand years ago, settling mainly in what is now the town of Buxton. However, the arrival of Europeans in the 1500's, along with illness and disease, caused the tribes' demise. In 1587, the English explorer Sir Walter Raleigh sent a group of colonists to establish a North American settlement. Raleigh asked that the new community be named Virginia, in

homage to Queen Elizabeth I, known as the "Virgin Queen."

As European ships explored the Atlantic coast, many stopped along the Outer Banks' shores to rest and restock supplies. Some of these explorers settled on the Outer Banks, and the islands' population blossomed in the early 1700's. Fishermen, traders, ranchers and entrepreneurs set up shop on the island, and by 1776, when the Revolutionary War was in full force, Outer Banks residents had to defend themselves against British soldiers, whose ships landed on the Outer Banks to pilfer food and supplies. Three years later, the Ocracoke Militia Company was formed to maintain the area's independence, and its 25 members successfully protected Ocracoke Inlet from the threat of British invasion.

By the time North Carolina became a state in 1789, over one

thousand residents lived on the Outer Banks. As maritime trade advanced and lighthouses were erected along the island's shores, word spread that the Outer Banks was an alluring summer destination. By 1900, nearly one thousand North Carolina visitors hit the Outer Banks beaches each day, and hundreds of businesses sprouted up to cater to this new populous.

In the 1930's, bridges were built to connect the Outer Banks to North Carolina mainland, bringing thousands more tourists to the sandy stretches of pristine beach. Cape Hatteras National Seashore was established in 1953 as the first national seashore in the United States, extending more than seventy miles from South Nags Head to Ocracoke Inlet. The National Seashore includes Hatteras Island and Ocracoke Island, along with seven villages and covering 30,000 acres.

Today, nearly seven million people visit the Outer Banks annually, but the islands aren't just popular in the summer. 26,000 people make the Outer Banks their year-round homes, and the autumn is a magical time to visit, with its golden yellow colors, agreeable temperatures and prime fishing conditions.

So, for those people who continue to wonder what makes the Outer Banks so special, it only takes one look at these exquisite photographs to discover an accurate **Portrait of the Outer Banks.**

"Testing the Water"
Frisco Beach at sunrise.

The sun breaks through the clouds on Frisco Beach.

left: The sun rises over Cape Hatteras Lighthouse.

above: Cape Hatteras Lighthouse, as seen from the Buxton Woods Nature Trail.

It's more than a lighthouse. It's a "Welcome Home" for weary travelers, and a protective guardian to the islanders. The Cape Hatteras Lighthouse is a symbol of the grace and strength of the Outer Banks.

Composed of over 1.25 million Philadelphia baked bricks, the Cape Hatteras Lighthouse remains North America's tallest brick lighthouse at 206 feet mean sea level. Although 269 spiral steps might sound like an awfully steep climb, thousands of visitors manage to find the trek surprisingly manageable—even peaceful. With the Atlantic Ocean lapping 1,600 feet from one side of the structure and Hatteras' famed dunes stretching past the other, only the black and white striped lighthouse's unyielding strength outshines its solitude and beauty.

Alexander Hamilton and Thomas Jefferson were responsible for the placement of Cape Hatteras' original lighthouse, built in 1803. Jefferson dubbed the coast the "Graveyard of the Atlantic" to describe the treacherous conditions that arose when the warm Gulf Stream clashed with the cold Labrador Current. Over 500 ships from several nations sank along the Cape Hatteras National Seashore during treks along the Seaboard.

At 90 feet, the original sandstone lighthouse's weak whale oil-powered lens was referred to as the "worst light in the world," and the building's structure cracked quickly due to frequent Nor'easters. In 1851, Lieutenant H.K. Davenport of the mail steamer Cherokee complained, "Cape Hatteras Light, upon the most dangerous point on our whole coast, is a very poor concern."

The generation of a national Lighthouse Board in 1852 allowed for improvements in Cape Hatteras' ineffective lighthouse. The tower was raised to 150 feet, and the Union forces fitted it with a first order Fresnel lens during the war, which amplified the oil wick flame to project further and more steadily.

Unfortunately, the new lighthouse suffered a lamentable fate when Confederate soldiers made off with the lens in 1861. Even though Hatteras was able to get the Lighthouse up and running again the following year, the structure was in poor condition and the Lighthouse Board recommended a new tower for Cape Hatteras.

In 1870, at a cost of over $150,000, the current tower was built on a floating foundation approximately 1,800 feet from the ocean. But the current changed over time, and by 1998, the structure stood only 120 feet from the water.

Sandbags, rubble and artificial seaweed were placed between the ocean and the lighthouse to keep the erosion to a minimum and the Park Service attempted to renourish the beach to prevent further erosion. But, by the 1980's, it was clear that the lighthouse would have to be relocated to avoid destruction.

On June 17, 1999, the lighthouse was moved the first ten feet, resting on the steel beam foundation that temporarily replaced its granite and mortar base. With the aid of hydraulic power, the moving crew was able to cover more and more ground each day, and the 2,900 foot move was completed by July 9th, just 23 days after it had begun.

Once again, the Cape Hatteras Lighthouse was ready to go to work again. And positioned three feet higher than at its previous location, it is able to perform its job even more efficiently—the beacon can now be seen a full 24 miles out to sea, helping millions of seamen navigate the rough waters of the Atlantic.

The Frisco Coast.

A pier overlooking the Atlantic at Nags Head.

Nags Head wakes up from one of the Outer Banks' storms.

Though the Outer Banks is the home of some of the most picturesque and most powerful lighthouses in the world, many other factors are involved when ships are navigating the Atlantic Coast. And no other component is more significant and foreboding than the notorious Outer Banks storms.

The Great Hurricane of 1899, also known as San Ciriaco, was one of the most devastating storms of the Nineteenth Century. Reports at the time speculated that nearly every house on Ocracoke was damaged, and that over thirty homes were destroyed. Boasting twenty to thirty-foot waves, San Ciriaco did its part to begin the nation's careful watch of the Outer Banks coast in late summer.

The Great Atlantic Hurricane struck Hatteras on September 14, 1944, and its 110 mile-per-hour winds managed to damage nearly 800 buildings.

And the Outer Banks received a double dose just before the Millennium. Hurricane Dennis blew through the Atlantic in September of 1999, though by the time it reached the Outer Banks on September 4, it had been downgraded to a tropical storm,

"Reverence for nature is what brought me here, and no act of nature will ever cause me to leave."

carrying 45-mile-per-hour winds. It hovered off the coast for seven days, beating the beach incessantly. It caused so much flooding that the Pamlico Sound and the Atlantic Ocean actually merged on the island between Buxton and Avon. Flooding caused the bulk of the storm's damaged, which was amplified less than two weeks later when Hurricane Floyd made a call on Hatteras. Though the storm's eye was not particularly close to the Outer Banks, its rain caused

more difficulty in rebuilding after Dennis' visit.

Yes, storms will continue to visit the Outer Banks, but, as one islander put it, "Reverence for nature is what brought me here, and no act of nature will ever cause me to leave."

As a result of the constant tumult in the Atlantic, the Outer Banks has long maintained a strong lifesaving program. The staggering number of shipwrecks off the Outer Banks in the Nineteenth Century caused the United States Lifesaving Service to establish the Chicamacomico Lifesaving Station in 1874. Located in Rodanthe, the station was one of the most complete lifesaving service/Coast Guard Station complexes on the Atlantic Coast.

That same year, six more lifesaving stations were built on the Outer Banks, located at Jones' Hill, Caffey's Inlet, Nags Head, Kitty Hawk, Oregon Inlet, and Little Kinnakeet.

In dangerous surf, the rescues were made with the help of "Lyle Guns," which were bronze cannons that fired floatation devices to victims. A "breeches buoy" was then lowered down to the troubled ship, which allowed the victim to settle into the attached "breeches," or pants, and hang onto the lifesaving ring while being pulled to shore. In 1899, during the San Ciriaco Hurricane, the entire crew of the three-masted schooner, Minnie Bergen, was saved this way.

The more sensational rescues were made by daring lifesaving crews rowing out to the victims in oar-powered surf boats.

Perhaps the most famous rescue occurred in August of 1918, when the British tanker Mirlo was struck by a torpedo fired by a German Submarine U-117. Chicamacomico Station Captain John Allen Midgett and his crew navigated their motor-powered surfboat through the fiery oil-slicked waters. As barrels of gasoline exploded on the Mirlo, Midgett and his crew rescued the six occupants of an overturned lifeboat, and over an exhausting six-hour period, helped 36 more crew members ashore.

Surfmen assigned to beach patrol were responsible for standing watch along seven miles of shoreline, either on foot or on horseback, during their shifts. If they saw a ship in distress, they lit a Coston signal (similar to a red flare) to ensure that help was on the way, then dispatched the appropriate lifesaving device.

Lifesaving stations in the Oregon Inlet and Ocracoke are still active today, though the Chicamacomico station was abandoned in 1954. Its station and boathouse still stand today as testaments to the heroes who so bravely operated them.

Chicamacomico Lifesaving Station.

above: View from the Lifesaving Station tower.

right: Looking into a barn at Chicamacomico Lifesaving Station.

left: Preparing the pulley system for the breeches buoy system at Chicamacomico. *Watercolor*

above: Hauling the breeches buoy back to shore at Chicamacomico. *Watercolor*

Coastline along Buxton Woods in the early
morning.

above: Cape Hatteras Lighthouse at sunrise.

right: The sun starts to rise over Cape Hatteras Lighthouse.

left: Surfers enjoy this spot by Cape Hatteras Lighthouse, which offers peaceful, yet challenging, sunrise surf conditions.

above: A kayaker paddles across Pamlico Sound toward Cape Hatteras Lighthouse.

above: A flying seagull can be spied more closely from this vantage point at the top of Cape Hatteras Lighthouse.

right: Cape Hatteras Lighthouse after a summer storm.

To conquer it all…
You must be proud
and stand tall

above: Cape Hatteras Lighthouse rests after its 2,900-foot move in the summer of 1999.

right: The path that led Hatteras Light to its new destination.

Cape Hatteras Lighthouse on its new
foundation in 1999.

Beach with moon still visible during early
morning sunrise.

Needless to say, the Outer Banks' Lifesaving Stations did not yet exist in the Eighteenth Century, when the waters of North Carolina's coast were dubbed the "Graveyard of the Atlantic." It is estimated that over one thousand ships met their demise on the coast of North Carolina, many of which sank within sight of the Outer Banks.

From the time that America was settled, our nation's commerce depended upon the familiar wooden sailing ships which frequently traveled up and down the Atlantic coast. Coastal trade routes led these vessels past the Outer Banks, often considered the most treacherous leg of the trek.

The infamous Diamond Shoals were only the first hurdle in safely passing North Carolina's barrier islands. To this day, the Shoals are known as an insidious, ever-changing series of underwater sandbars stretching eight miles from Cape Hatteras. For those sailors knowledgeable enough to safely navigate the Shoals without running aground, the next challenge was navigating the area's shifting water current.

Uniting just off of Cape Hatteras' shores, the cold Labrador Current and the warm Gulf Stream create a nasty current which can be a formidable task for a ship's navigator. The most advantageous option is for the vessel to sail close to the Outer Banks, which, in the old days, was notorious for its weak or nonexistent lighthouses. To make matters worse, many boats have been taken by surprise by the region's dreaded hurricanes and Nor'easters.

The Outer Banks' natural perils weren't the only reasons that so many ships faced their final destinies in North Carolina—pirates and wartime gunfire were also responsible for sinking many boats. Shipwreck souvenirs abound on Hatteras Island's beaches, and many beachcombers proudly display collections of formerly sunken treasures.

Several buried ships are seasonally revealed off North Carolina's coast during storms or shifts in tide, and some can even be seen during normal weather conditions when the tide changes. Divers often make vacations out of exploring the Outer Banks' sunken ships, and many fish make the vessels their homes.

left: A fisherman's boat berthed at Oden's Dock in Hatteras Village.

below: "Almost Finished" Crabbers return from a successful early morning excursion.

left: "Sunrise Fishing"
Early morning risers surf fishing along Outer Banks coast.

right: A pelican stands above marshy waters in Hatteras Village.

Sometimes it's the sight of a sole fly fisherman angling off Frisco at sunrise. Other times, it's a group of commercial fishermen headed out toward the Gulf Stream. Regardless of the fishing style or time of year, it's inevitable that someone, somewhere, is fishing off the Outer Banks.

The Outer Banks boasts some of the greatest fishing anywhere—both in the size of fish and the variety of breeds. Records are shattered as lines are pulled out of the water. Take, for example, the 1,142 pound blue marlin captured in 1974 and the World-record-breaking red drum caught off Avon. And, for off-season oddities, you can't beat the 2,200 pounds of crab that Ocracoke

native James Gaskill caught in March of 1984—an impressive catch any time, but especially before spring begins.

Gaskill, who has earned his living as a fisherman since 1979, attributes the optimal fishing conditions at least partially to the Gulf Stream, the 50-mile wide flow of warm water where fish of all species flock to seek refuge from the often cold Atlantic waters. The Gulf Stream also releases warm pockets of water, which provide comfortable spots for mahi-mahi and tuna, and often allow fishermen to score huge catches. Gaskill also believes that the Outer Banks' distance from heavily polluted areas contributes to the superb fishing conditions.

Perhaps the most dependable fishing attraction of the Outer Banks is the surf fishing, which is said to be unmatched. Throughout the summer, even beginners can catch dinner in the surf. When the water is cool, anglers regularly pull in channel bass from 30 to 60 pounds, along with trout and jumbo bluefish.

The beauty of surf fishing is that even if a fisherman doesn't happen to catch anything, the time is never wasted—a visit to the Outer Banks' surf is said to be one of the most relaxing trips imaginable.

above: A fishing boat rests after a morning spent crabbing and fishing.

right: Seagulls in Hatteras Village.

above: "Time Out"
A fishing boat in Hatteras Village.

right: "Safari"
A boat docked at a Hatteras Village
fish house.

top left: "Fish House"
The view across Pamlico Sound from Hatteras Village.

bottom left: "Bicycles"
Bicycles parked along Oden's Dock.

above: "Easy-Does-It"
A fisherman preparing to work on his boat at Oden's Dock.

Truly beautiful and truly kind
In this light happiness is what I find
—Christine M. Drapala

Feel my peace
It is never broken
For this is my peace
This is my token…
To life.
—Christine M. Drapala

Part of Ocracoke's allure is the fact that it's only accessible by ferry or air.

It's difficult to consider a fishing trip to the Outer Banks without a visit to Ocracoke, known for its history of hardy fishermen. In fact, part of Ocracoke's allure is the fact that it's only accessible by ferry or air.

Tales endure that Ocracoke's most famous visitor, the pirate Blackbeard, stashed treasure along the North Carolina Coast. Each summer, the quaint fishing village is transformed into a popular tourist destination, still overflowing with the Seventeenth Century charm that made it known as the Outer Banks' most picturesque location.

Ocracoke was documented by cartographers as early as 1585, when English colonists landed in Ocracoke Inlet. Legend has it that Blackbeard, the crafty pirate known for terrorizing merchant ships, used what is now known as "Teach's Hole," a North Carolina inlet, as a docking point between his Atlantic Coast pursuits.

It's difficult to know whether Ocracoke's wild ponies were roaming the island during Blackbeard's time. No one may ever know whether the horses came from shipwrecks, early Spanish explorers or English settlers. The ponies were known to wander Ocracoke Island throughout the Eighteenth and Nineteenth Centuries, and were often seen roaming along the dunes and splashing in the salty Atlantic surf. Several of the horses remain on the island, fenced into a seven-mile range superintended by the National Park Service.

Another of Ocracoke's most famous sites is the British Cemetery. In 1942, the 170-foot H.M.S. *Bedforshire* was blasted by German torpedo fire, killing all 37 sailors on board. The ship sank 38 miles south of Ocracoke, and four of the bodies washed ashore on Ocracoke. The Island's devoted residents did not hesitate to offer a plot of community cemetery land to commemorate the seamen's bravery. The grassy area is, like all of Ocracoke, a symbol of class, with a white picket fence and a British flag surrounding the headstones, which are lovingly placed under a collection of trees.

Ocracoke Island is still famous as the site of Blackbeard's final confrontation, but it is known to those who have been there as a charming village with Nineteenth Century appeal and Twenty-First Century amenities.

left: Ferries stationed at the Hatteras Village ferry landing.

top: Aerial view of Ocracoke Island. Teach's Hole, where Blackbeard once sat in wait for treasure, is in the upper left of the photo. From here he could look out between the inlet of Ocracoke and Portsmouth as ships moved along the coast.

bottom: Aerial view of Hatteras and Ocracoke at sunset.

Ocracoke's most famous and longest enduring resident is the Ocracoke Lighthouse…

Blackbeard aside, Ocracoke's most famous and longest enduring resident is the Ocracoke Lighthouse, built in 1823. The oldest active lighthouse in North Carolina, the current tower replaced the original wooden structure on Shell Castle Island, which was built in 1803 and was destroyed by lightning just 15 years later.

The 75-foot Lighthouse is constructed entirely of white-washed bricks, with an octagonal lantern holding a stationary beam of 8,000 candlepower visible up to 14 miles out to sea. Even the quaint two-story double keepers' quarters is still occupied by park employees.

Though the lighthouse is not open for climbing, visitors still enjoy trips to the area, with its charming wooden walkway and white fence.

The lighthouse is simple, beautiful and powerful, just like Ocracoke itself.

Aerial view of Ocracoke Lighthouse.
A collection of photos, aerial and ground,
of lighthouses along the east coast.

Sunsets in Silver Lake at Ocracoke. Many blue water sailors stop here to relax and enjoy the island.

Historians speculate that Blackbeard was born Edward Drummond around the year 1680, and later called himself Edward Teach or Thatch. He could read and write, and records show that he corresponded with merchants, indicating that he must have been born into a fairly well-off family.

Blackbeard's reputation began when he was the captain of *The Concorde,* a ship containing forty guns and several small cannons. He attacked the large merchant ship the *Great Allen* off St. Vincent, and after a long struggle, Blackbeard pillaged the cargo and burned and sank the ship.

Thereafter, Blackbeard became known as a fearless pirate, and he fashioned his appearance to match his reputation. He was tall and broad, with a bushy black beard that he often braided into little pigtails and tied with colorful ribbons to get attention before a battle. He wore pistols and daggers on a belt, and a sling across his chest held six pistols.

Rumor had it that Blackbeard was friendly with North Carolina's Governor, Charles Eden. Historians believe that Eden looked the other way when

Blackbeard was terrorizing ships, and that the Governor even shared some of Blackbeard's booty.

In May of 1718, Blackbeard's reign of terror came to a peak when he blocked Charleston, South Carolina's port for a week, capturing gold, slaves, and other valuables. One week later, while sailing up the Atlantic coast on a French ship that he had captured and renamed the *Queen Anne's Revenge,* Blackbeard ran aground. After unloading the ship's treasure onto another of his vessels, the *Queen Anne's Revenge* sank off the coast of North Carolina.

Six months later, Blackbeard met his death in a bloody battle off of Ocracoke Island where he often perched in "Teach's Hole," a cove from which he watched ships travel through the inlet. However, tales of his sunken treasure have lasted for over 250 years, while divers, scavengers and archaeolo-

gists alike have searched for his ship.

Fortune smiled on those who pursued the *Queen Anne's Revenge,* when underwater archaeologists believed that they discovered the ship off Morehead City, North Carolina in 1997. A casualty of the "Graveyard of the Atlantic", the ship yielded several artifacts, including a foot-tall bronze bell bearing the date 1709, forty cannons, and a 24-pound cannonball.

Divers continue to excavate the ship, which is undergoing inspection to verify that it is, indeed, the flagship of the infamous pirate. Tales and speculation about Blackbeard can still be heard along the coast of the Outer Banks, not only the final resting place of the *Queen Anne's Revenge,* but of Blackbeard himself. Perhaps his long-sought treasure will be the next items to turn up along North Carolina's shores...

"Bicycles II"
Bicycles at Oden's Dock.

"Day's Catch"
Weighing the day's catch at a dock on
Ocracoke Island.

Commercial fishermen finishing up a
day's work on Ocracoke Island.

top left: "Day End"
A boat docked at an Ocracoke fish house.

bottom left: "Latitude"
Latitude, Ocracoke.

above: "Ocracoke Light"
Ocracoke Lighthouse, towering above the harbor.

A boat docked in one of the
many inlets on Ocracoke Island.

"Sailing"
Sailing off Ocracoke Island.
Watercolor

Graveyard behind Ocracoke Lighthouse.
Watercolor

The sunset, as seen from Ocracoke Island Village.

Wildlife is abundant on Ocracoke Island.

"Follow Me"
Skimmers to Teach's Hole off Ocracoke.

"Ocracoke Island Sailboats"

"Sailing II"

Coastline along Ocracoke Island.

above: Aerial view of Portsmouth Island.

right: Cape Lookout

While Portsmouth Village stands at the Northeast end of Cape Lookout National Seashore, another historic landmark remains at the opposite end—the Cape Lookout Lighthouse.

The original Cape Lookout Lighthouse was first lit in 1812, and, at 96-feet tall, its red and white horizontal strips were, originally, hard to miss.

But following complaints that the lighthouse was too short and not bright enough, a new, 163-foot red brick lighthouse was built in 1859. Its first-order Fresnel lens could be seen eighteen miles out to sea on a clear day.

During the Civil War, Confederate troops tried to destroy the lighthouse, but their attempts only damaged the Fresnel lens, which was replaced by a temporary third-order lens until the original lens was repaired.

The black and white diamond checkerboard pattern, which was painted on the tower in 1873, allowed seafarers to navigate easily in the daytime as well as at night: the black diamonds face north and south, while the white diamonds run east and west.

Today, the lighthouse is powered by two 1,000-watt airport

beacon lights, each of which produces an 800,000 candlepower beam. The short flash, which appears every fifteen seconds, can be seen twenty miles out to sea during good weather.

Though the lighthouse is closed to the public, the keepers' quarters can be visited each spring, summer and fall. It's a

peaceful trip for anyone wishing to visit one of the most richly populated areas of the Outer Banks, in terms of wildlife and nature.

above: Walking over this dock is like taking a step in time. It leads to the center of the abandoned town of Portsmouth.

right: Wildlife on Portsmouth Island.

1753, and it quickly became one of the most important ports on the Atlantic Coast. At that time, Ocracoke Inlet was a dominant trade route for shippers delivering goods to significant North Carolina ports. Those heavy ships were unable to navigate through the shallow Outer Banks waters, so they transferred their cargo to lighter draft boats based in Portsmouth. This allowed Portsmouth to grow tremendously, and by 1860, it was home to 685 residents.

Many of those islanders fled at the outset of the Civil War, while others left after a deeper inlet in Hatteras replaced the shallowing Ocracoke Inlet. Some Portsmouth inhabitants began to fish for a living, though by 1956, only 17 residents remained. The shallow waters, along with extreme flooding after a series of harsh storms, made the island an undesirable home, and by 1971, Portsmouth was completely abandoned.

But the village remaining in Portsmouth still stands, giving a glimpse of how this ghost town once thrived. Listed on the National Register of Historic Places, Portsmouth is one of the great reminders of America's past.

Unlike the Lost Colony, there is no mystery surrounding the slow abandonment of Portsmouth Island, a once lively sea village which began literally settling into the Atlantic by the early 1900's.

The North Carolina Assembly created Portsmouth Village in

The Portsmouth Graveyard, as seen from the town's sole post office.

top: The Portsmouth Post Office.
bottom: The Portsmouth Graveyard.

right: Old outhouse. *Watercolor*

The Portsmouth Church steeple. *Watercolor*

top: Reflection along a stream.

bottom: Tiny lizard, one of the many Islands wildlife.

The view from inside the church on
Portsmouth Island, looking out on
Portsmouth's former residences.

top: An abandoned barn at the Portsmouth Lifesaving Station.

bottom: One of the island's many inhabitants.

right: The grounds and old barn of the Lifesaving Station, as seen from the Station's observation tower.

As Nor'easters and hurricanes charge the Outer Banks, evidence of the past appears as shells, driftwood and marine plants wash onto the shore. Humans and animals learn to follow Mother Nature's cues.

Acres of salt marshes carve through the Outer Banks, creating a haven for the marine life that shuns the Atlantic's thunderous waves. The island's many sounds supply freshwater plant and animal species with a place to flourish, while the Gulf Stream keeps vegetation moving toward the Outer Banks, allowing the "circle of life" to continue.

Over 500 national wildlife refuges exist in the United States, and two of them are located on the Outer Banks. Pea Island National Wildlife Refuge extends from Oregon Inlet to Rodanthe. Originally established in 1938 as a winter sanctuary for waterfowl, the Refuge contains 5,915 acres of ocean beach, barrier dunes, salt marshes, water ponds, tidal creeks and bays, along with 25,700 acres of Pamlico Sound Proclamation Boundary Waters. Nearly 400 species of birds frequent the Island, including some endan-

The Outer Banks has long been known as a enticing vacation spot for nature lovers. The accessibility of the Atlantic Ocean makes it a haven for beachcombers and offshore fishermen, while acres of untouched estuary offer sightings of rare marine life. Whale watching can be enjoyed in spring and winter, and visits to the many wildlife refuges allow for interaction with birds, reptiles, amphib-

ians, and countless mammals, not to mention the untarnished beauty of wildflowers and trees. Endangered species visit the Outer Banks, where they, too, enjoy finding refuge.

As the indomitable force that created the barrier islands, nature continues to reshape the Outer Banks on a daily basis. Winter waves move sand between dunes, beach and sandbars, while gentler gered species such as peregrine falcons, piping plovers and bald eagles.

Other animals besides birds also flourish on Pea Island, including loggerhead sea turtles, Carolina salt marsh snakes, frogs, lizards, bats, moles, fox, raccoons, minks, deer and otter.

West of Roanoke lies Alligator River National Wildlife Refuge, established in 1984 to preserve the environmentally complex wetlands which are home to thousands of animals and plants. The Refuge contains over 152,000 acres between Croatan Sound and Alligator River, and is home to black bear, deer, wood ducks, owls, waterfowl, alligators, falcons, and even red wolves, which had been declared extinct before their population was rebuilt at Alligator River in the 1980's. The Refuge is popular with human visitors as well, since it contains wildlife trails, canoe and kayak launches, and hunting and fishing areas.

Legend has it that Jockey's Ridge State Park got its name from early Outer Banks residents who captured wild ponies and raced them on the base of the dunes. It is a logical explanation, considering that Jockey's Ridge is the tallest natural sand dune system in the Eastern United States. At 80 to 100 feet in height, the offshore wind constantly shifts the dune's sands back and forth. At the base of the dune, an estuarine environment serves as a rich habitat for plant and animal life. Species such as bayberry, red cedar, hickory and live oak can be found in the drier areas of the park, while the estuary offers sawgrass, black needlebrush, saltmarsh cordgrass and duck potato. Animals enjoy visiting the pools of water in the early morning hours, and hikers have encountered fox, rabbits, frogs and waterfowl, among many others.

The Nags Head Woods preserve contains 1,400 acres of maritime forest and over 300 species of plant life. The forest is covered with violets, ferns, bamboo, evergreen, pines, and scores of other botanical wonders. Reptiles, amphibians, waterfowl and such mammals as raccoons, fox, deer and opossum also call Nags Head Woods home.

North Carolina's largest maritime forest is Buxton Woods, located on Hatteras Island. Boasting 3,000 acres, Buxton Woods is an especially moist environment, as it supplies the area from Avon to Hatteras Island with drinking water. Both deciduous and evergreen maritime forests flourish, and Buxton Woods is home to the Outer Banks' most diverse population.

Bird watchers and whale watchers alike will swear by the Outer Banks' synergism with nature. The island's bounty of natural wonders far outweighs the occasional Nor'easter or hurricane. The weather is, after all, what created the Outer Banks, one of the country's most elaborate natural sanctuaries.

Even the modes of transportation leading on and off Hatteras are charming. The three-mile-long Oregon Inlet Bridge offers free fishing catwalks and an unparalleled view, while the Hatteras-Ocracoke Ferry provides not only a lift from one island to another, but also allows passengers to enjoy a forty-minute journey along Blackbeard's path. Often in the summer, more people can be seen riding the ferry with their bicycles than their cars.

It's just another sign of how the Outer Banks represents a simpler time, where natural beauty reigns and visitors long to take a mental snapshot of one last sunset...

above: Sunrise at Cape Lookout.
right: Aerial view of Cape Lookout.

left: Stormy weather in Frisco.
above: Cape Lookout.

The Chicamacomico ferry boat makes
its way from Ocracoke Island to
Hatteras. *Watercolor*

More than a half mile from the Atlantic Ocean and nesting in a field of grass, Bodie Island Lighthouse stands as a monument to its strength in overcoming perils. Much like the Outer Banks itself, Bodie Island Light has fallen victim to North Carolina's natural hazards, yet it remains just as pristine and unaffected as the island itself.

Towering 156 feet and 214 steps above North Carolina's sandy shoals, the lighthouse's black and white horizontal stripes are a welcome signal to the thousands of Cape Hatteras National Seashore visitors.

In 1837, the Federal Government dispatched a cutter to examine the North Carolina coastline for possible lighthouse locations. Lieutenant Napoleon L. Coste reported back that Bodie Island would be an ideal spot for a light, and wrote, "More vessels are lost there than on any other part of our coast." Congress funded the original Bodie Island Lighthouse in 1837, but land purchasing difficulties delayed construction until 1846.

Guiding visitors through Oregon Inlet, the 54-foot structure was ill-fated from the beginning. The combination of an unstable foundation and treacherous weather conditions caused the lighthouse to crack and tilt. In 1859, an 80-foot tower was constructed on firmer ground, but two years later, Confederate troops filled the lighthouse with explosives and destroyed it in an attempt to avoid the Union's use of the lighthouse as an observation post.

The current lighthouse was built on fifteen acres of land in 1872 and sustained only minor damage when a flock of geese crashed into the lantern shortly after its first lighting. Repairs allowed the original lens, which now uses an incandescent electric lamp as its principal source of light, to continue burning. Emitting 13,000 candlepower, the beam boasts a nineteen mile range, keeping sailors steadily on track through the Inlet.

Visitors find a certain serenity at the light and its adjacent keeper's quarters, which convey the timeless beauty and simplicity of the Outer Banks' early years.

Aerial view of Bodie Island Lighthouse.

"Peaceful"

Cape Hatteras Lighthouse rising tall at sunrise.

above: Pea Island National Wildlife Refuge with reflection of morning sun off the airplane's wing.

right: Oregon Inlet at sunrise—fishing boats make their way out to sea.

Left: Bodie Island Lighthouse.

above: Lifesaving Station, Oregon Inlet.

More than 400 species of birds live on Pea Island.

above: Bodie Island Light at sunrise.

right: Aerial view of Pea Island looking toward Bodie Lighthouse.

In 1910, the Lighthouse Board decided to take action. After 49 ships had been grounded over a 22-year stretch between

The Currituck Beach Lighthouse first glowed on December 1, 1875, with a beacon that could be seen eleven miles out to sea.

Cape Henry and Bodie Island Lighthouse, the Lighthouse Board chose to build the Currituck Beach Lighthouse in Corolla, at the northern end of the Outer Banks.

The Lighthouse first glowed on December 1, 1875, with a beacon that could be seen eleven miles out to sea. To distinguish it from the Outer Banks' other lighthouses, Currituck Beach was not painted, and still remains in its original red brick state.

The mineral oil lamp that first gave the lighthouse its glow has been replaced with an electric light, which continues to illuminate its original first-order lens, still in operation today. Visitors can climb Currituck's 214 steps for a view of the island, which is particularly beautiful since a restoration of the tower and grounds in the 1980's. The project was led by the Outer Banks Conservationists, the same group that has been instrumental in saving the wild ponies of Corolla....

Bodie Island Lighthouse can be seen nineteen miles out to sea.

Currituck Light in Corolla.

...When the Spanish explorers visited the North Carolina coast in the early 1500's, they brought a variety of livestock, including horses bred in what is now Puerto Rico. When conflicts arose between the Spanish and the Native Americans, the Spaniards fled, leaving their livestock on the Outer Banks. But, according to Spanish Mustang researcher Dale Burrus, there is a hole in the time-line of the history of those horses, because they cannot be traced between 1521 and 1584. "The Spanish Mustangs present today can be traced back to 1584, with the settling of what's now referred to as the Lost Colony," says Burrus.

The members of the Lost Colony bought their horses and other livestock in present-day Santo Domingo and Puerto Rico, and set up their community on the Outer Banks. "At that point, the horses were known as the Spanish Marsh Ponies," says Burrus, "and they weren't a pri-mary interest of the settlers, but they were necessary to work the farm and help round up the more important livestock, like the cows and sheep."

Burrus points out that for a long time, historians didn't link

Mustang ponies grazing north of Currituck Light.

the horses to the Lost Colony, because they couldn't figure out why British settlers would own Spanish horses. "But," he says, "the English knew these horses were already acclimated to this hemisphere, coming out of South America, so it is logical that the English would buy the horses in the Americas."

When the Lost Colony settlers disappeared, the livestock remained. The barrier islands that comprise the Outer Banks are like natural pens: with water sur-rounding all sides, the animals simply cannot wander away, so the mustangs remained.

Recent DNA studies on Corolla's mustangs have confirmed

the horses' Spanish origins, and verified the fact that the horses' isolation has caused them to become their own, distinctive breed.

When a paved road was opened to the public in 1984 in Corolla, the horses were thrust out of their natural state, and became tourist attractions. About 15 of them were killed on the roads, vic-tims of car accidents. Since then, the conservationists have moved them to a safer place where the horses can still keep the families intact. "Today," says Burrus, "there are probably not more than 50 Spanish Mustangs left in Corolla."

The 214-stair climb to the top of Currituck Beach Lighthouse is worth the effort. The view from the top is truly breathtaking.

A Great Blue Heron rests near Currituck
Beach Lighthouse.

bottom: Kayakers near Currituck Light.
Watercolor

Aerials of Currituck Light.

Aerial of Wright Brothers Monument.
Watercolor

Hang gliding is one of the most popular sports on the Outer Banks, and it makes sense that the islands would boast near-perfect conditions: high, soft dunes for launching, gentle breezes to carry the glider through the air, and miles of water and nature below, making for a scenic flight. In fact, two enterprising brothers thought that the area was so perfect that they used it to test their experimental homemade glider in the year 1900.

Orville and Wilbur Wright were builders from childhood, always curious about how to invent and improve machinery. In 1888 they built a printing press and worked as publishers in Ohio. Four years later they opened a bicycle repair shop, and began assembling bicycles with tools that they had crafted. But they were fascinated with flight, and studied the writings and feats of engineers who had experimented with gliders. The brothers crafted their own glider in 1899 which tested a new

method that involved warping the wings to achieve lateral control, an idea that Wilbur discovered after observing birds in flight.

Marker commemorating the Wright Brothers' first flight in Kitty Hawk.

above: Sunset behind sand dune at Jockey's Ridge State Park.

right: Flight line of first flight, with hangar and monument in background.

In 1900, Orville and Wilbur took their 17-foot glider to North Carolina. They chose the site at Kill Devil Hills, between Kitty Hawk and Nags Head, because it provided isolation, high dunes, strong winds and soft landings in the sand. After launching their glider, the brothers were disappointed to see that it operated more like a kite than a plane, but they carefully recorded their findings, concluding that the aeronautical data that they had relied upon and studied was incorrect.

Throughout 1901 and 1902, the brothers experimented with the effects of air pressure on various wing surfaces and built a new, more efficient glider. At their Kitty Hawk camp, they tested the new glider, which boasted 32-foot wings and was balanced by a human pilot, rather than a built-in engineering device. The Wrights were more successful this time, concluding that the addition of a propeller would create the world's first working airplane.

Orville and Wilbur designed a lightweight, gasoline-powered engine and a rotary wing propeller, and positioned their new

inventions onto their forty-foot, 605 pound *Flyer*. The brothers perfected the airplane at Kill Devil Hills, where they tested *Flyer* for the first time.

On December 17, 1903, at 10:35 am, the Wright brothers made history. Orville climbed onto the plane, and, with Wilbur running alongside, the flyer lifted off the ground into 27 mph winds. As Orville later wrote, "This flight lasted only twelve seconds, but it was nevertheless the first flight in the history of the world in which a machine carrying a man had raised itself by its own power into the air in full flight, had sailed forward without reduction of speed and had finally landed at a point as high as that

from which it started." Orville and Wilbur continued testing the plane for the remainder of the day, and Wilbur flew an impressive 852 feet, logging a record 59 seconds in the air.

The world's first true pilots shared their news with the rest of the world, creating a place in history for themselves, and for Kill Devil Hills. Though the Wright brothers' North Carolina campsite was modest, it was the Outer Banks' land that help them create magic. The site of their first flight is marked by the Wright Brothers National Memorial at Kill Devil Hills, where visitors can retrace history and discover the pride that the Outer Banks had in making world history.

Elizabeth II.

In 1587, Sir Walter Raleigh sent a group of colonists, led by London cartographer John White, to establish an English settlement in North America. White took the group, including his daughter Eleanor and her husband Ananias Dare, to Roanoake Island, where White's granddaughter, Virginia, was born.

Nine days after Virginia arrived, John White returned to England to retrieve food and supplies. A war broke out between England and Spain before White could make it back to the Outer Banks, so his return to Roanoke was delayed for four years. By the time he sailed back to North Carolina, the colony had disappeared, and the inhabitants, including White's granddaughter Virginia Dare, were never found.

The fate of those early settlers remains a mystery to modern historians, who continue to debate whether the colonists left to explore the North Carolina mainland, were killed by Native Americans, or were lost at sea. A living memorial called the Elizabethan Gardens stands on Roanoke Island, featuring replicas from 16th Century Windsor Castle and tributes to the lost colonists.

The only clue was the word "Croton" carved into a tree. Many believe that it was a message about where the settlers were going, while claims that it may have been a warning signal have been widely disputed.

It almost seems unfathomable to imagine what led the "Lost Colony" settlers away from the Outer Banks. Granted, in the 16th Century, there was no Cape Hatteras Light, no Oden's Dock, and no ferry. But the essential elements that make the Outer Banks such a breathtaking, serene place already existed when Sir Walter Raleigh sent John White and his crew to "Virginia."

Though at that point the island wasn't known as the Cape Hatteras National Seashore, it already had the same elements of paradise that make it such a special place today—quiet, undisturbed beaches, a vast array of wildlife and fish, and breathtaking sunsets.

Even as we begin a new millennium, the Outer Banks remains unaffected by the mass development taking place around the rest of the country. In fact, some people say there isn't a spot on the island where they *can't* hear the waves breaking on the shore.

On the Outer Banks, there will always be someone reeling in a fish…someone watching the birds skim across the water…and someone sitting by the water's edge. Because even lifelong residents of the Outer Banks have

trouble looking away from the hypnotic beauty of this island.

So here's to hoping that if the "Lost Colony" somehow looked down over the Outer Banks today, they would still recognize it as the pristine, tranquil island where they lived over 400 years ago.

Sunset on the Outer Banks.

As the sun sets, I feel at rest...
To have been at work all day in the sea
And now be at rest and enjoy the beauty around me
—Holly Noel Josephina

Feel the peace as the sun goes to sleep
Feel the slight breeze as the night starts to peak
Enjoy the colors and company of others
As you relax in your seat as the sun goes to sleep

—Bobby